Venus and Other Losses

Lucia Galloway

Plain View Press
P. O. 42255
Austin, TX 78704

plainviewpress.net
sb@plainviewpress.net
512-441-2452

Copyright Lucia Galloway, 2010. All rights reserved.
ISBN: 978-1-935514-30-5
Library of Congress Number: 2009943153

Cover art © 2007, "Places of the Heart #6" by Prilla Smith Brackett
Cover design by Susan Bright

for John, Maggie, Laurie, and Charlotte

Acknowledgments

Grateful acknowledgment is made to the publications in which versions of the following poems first appeared (those published prior to 2005 appeared under the author's legal name, Lucia Dick or Lucia Anne Dick):

"Roller Skating with Walt Whitman" in *The Crimson Crane*; "Autumn Equinox," "Ceremony," "Our Turn," "Towards Evening, Overcast" and "Winter's Tales" in *Cumberland Poetry Review*; "Quince" in *Gertrude*; "Link" in *Her Mark, 2007*; "Urbane Pianos" in *Her Mark, 2009*; "Birdsong" and "Hymn Meters after Emily" in *The Lyric*; "Found Horses" in *The MacGuffin*; "I, Voyeur," "The Comtesse d'Haussonville with Nature Morte," "Jane Carlyle Laments," "Letters to Ralph Waldo Emerson from His Second Wife" and "Falling Asleep" in *Poemeleon*; "I Experience Agriculture," "Borrowed Landscape," "Bending Water" and "For a Woman Washing Vases" in *Poetry Midwest*; "Elsewhere" in *Prism Review*; "Ourselves, Afraid" in *Sierra Nevada College Review*; and "You, there" in *Verdad*. "Venus and Other Losses," "Soft Parts," "Meadowlands," "Modulations," "Poem without the Piano," "Playing Outside," "To a Washing Machine," "Benton's Hailstorm" and "Ginseng on Court Street" first appeared in my limited-edition chapbook, *Playing Outside* (Finishing Lines Press, 2005), some of the poems under different titles.

Thanks to Chris Abani, Richard Garcia, Frank Gaspar, and David Trinidad, my mentors in the Antioch MFA Program; and to Paul Muldoon, whose teaching got me started on the right path.

Thanks also to Lavina Blossom, Gayle Brandeis, Charlotte Davidson, Judy Kronenfeld, Frances McConnel, Ruth Nolan, Cati Porter, and Judith Terzi, and to Andrew Hudgins, Alan Shapiro, and Mark Strand, all of whom read drafts of many of these poems and offered valuable critique. Deep thanks to Maureen Alsop and Eloise Klein Healy, who read the entire manuscript and whose counsel proved invaluable in bringing this book to fruition.

Special thanks to John Dick, whose availability as a sounding board and a technical wizard helped me resolve many a dilemma.

Contents

I

Venus and Other Losses	9
Soft Parts	12
Link	14
Metonymy's Economy	15
Our Turn	16
A Grave and Orderly Array	17
Yellow Water	19
Siblings	21
Ourselves, Afraid	24
Meadowlands	25
Autumn Equinox	26
She Told Me Stories	27
History's Locomotive	28
Modulations	30
Poem without the Piano	32
Thirteen	33
Playing Outside	34
To a Washing Machine	36
Winter's Tales	39
To My Singing Partner	41
Birdsong	42

II

Tree Men	45
You, there	47
Elsewhere	49
I, Voyeur	50
The Comtesse d'Haussonville with *Nature Morte*	52
Jane Carlyle Laments	53
Letters to Ralph Waldo Emerson from His Second Wife	55
Hymn Meters, after Emily	57

III

We Are Occasional Like That	61
Benton's Hailstorm	62
Towards Evening, Overcast	63
Falling Asleep	64
Ceremony	66
Urbane Pianos	67
Trimaran	68
I Experience Agriculture	69
Quince	71
Borrowed Landscape	72
Bending Water	73
Ginseng on Court Street	74
In Eisenstadt, Visiting the Jewish Museum	77
Proving Ground	80
For a Woman Washing Vases	82
Instructions for the Lucia-let	83
Roller Skating with Walt Whitman	85
Found Horses	86

Notes   89

About the Author   91

I

*We lose everything, but make harvest
of the consequence it was to us.*
—Jack Gilbert

Venus and Other Losses

i

Dirt warm as ash recedes at a cavern's mouth
that Yorgos entered to escape the Aegean sun.
He squats in the cave's cool hall, he feels a knob,
begins to dig and gradually scrapes
the soil from her astonished torso
still hiding its lovely torque in the modest clay.

He bears the object in his sun-burnt arms—
his earthy gift—into the light. His sun and moon,
his Aphrodite. But she'll be taken from him
to illuminate a grand salon in the Louvre—
Venus de Milo, perfect, armless,
abiding the viewer's gaze.

ii

My own arm screaming from my cousin's
twisting it up behind my back.
(Are all boys such callow playmates?)
This same kid made me ride the handlebars
while he rode zigzag, fast
around the oval track, and I needed
the strength of both my arms
to keep from flying.

iii

Muscles in her legs and belly tense;
the gathers of her tunic press against
her thighs. Iris, the flying messenger, cropped
from the west pediment of the Parthenon,
alights without the help of either wings or arms
on the fake Acropolis erected
at the British Museum. Last night
I dreamt my infant daughter had been thrown
into a barrel, and I, armless,
could not rescue her.

iv

A son supported in his mother's arms,
dead across her lap—the Pietà.

v

The mother hovers near him, registering
his pain: her son, the climber, had cut off his arm
to cripple death. One hand pinned
beneath a boulder, he'd snapped the arm bones
with the other, sawed through radius and ulna,
like a cook disjointing chicken with a dull knife.

vi

I want to rub my broken arm with dirt
from the pit in the holy room where slings
and crutches line the walls. The Santuario
de Nuestro Señor. Amulets of tin some call
milagros are for sale on streets converging
on the place of healing—miniature legs and feet,
those little arms.

vii

Four arms of the dancing Shiva: two
to hold the drum and flame, a third
to gesture benediction. A fourth
to bend the sword.

Soft Parts

for Laurie

"I'm making slugs from snails," you said,
a deft blow from the rock in your hand
smashing down on the whorl of another shell
to liberate its naked occupant. You were just
four or five. We thought you precocious.

Did we think also of the body cast you'd worn
in babyhood to realign your hips and thighs?
Your tummy must have itched inside your plaster shell.
I think of the chafe of your ankles against the cuffs
of chalk and gauze, the rigid tights that sheathed your legs.

Snails take shelter in the vestibules of spiral shells,
coming out to make their transient, iridescent trails.
You couldn't slither out, although you'd use
your arms and feet, turtle-like, to move across the floor.

I couldn't even diaper you, take your ankles in one hand
to slide the folded cloth under your little bum,
but had to invent a way to fit the cut-down Pampers
into the oblong hole in the crotch of your cast.
I missed the stack of 4-ply cotton diapers,
lost track of the pink-headed diaper pins.

I lost the touch of bath water gloving my hands,
washing the fold of skin inside each baby thigh;
the nesting of you, damp and warm, against me, your shape
conforming to mine as I held you to my chest.
The hooded towel I'd toss around you—lost that too.

I keep this litany of what I lost because in no way
could I own the shell you kept around you. Not
experience your tenancy or penetrate its privacy:
the dark safety of your knees, their dimples cosseted.
Your hips and thighs arranged just so,
your buttocks pressed as smooth as pillows in a drawer.

Shells I know by their outer surfaces:
horny, hard to the touch, alien,
but to their owners, homes—yes, fortresses.
To bunker and body armor do small creatures
entrust their soft parts—the snails and turtles,
crabs and lobsters, beetles, armadillos.

And you, now in your adulthood, your shell
nearly invisible and paper-thin between us:
your letters durable and correct, even in their
girded irony, their carapace of wit. In parchment
envelopes they come, with my address
scripted in careful lines across the front.

Link

Something forming part of a chain:
a piece of metal bent. A missing segment of the armor,
the opening through which a lance's point can slay.
The loop of a necklace that breaks, letting
the jewel slip unnoticed off your neck. Also,
a joint of the body: a hip, an elbow, or a shoulder:
the meeting of the scapula and clavicle.
A rod or lever enlivening a machine.
A thing or person threading its way with
burdens: a river or a messenger.
A means of travel between two points: the
airport bus, a ferry boat across the sound.
The lone railroad across Siberia that connects Harbin
with Lake Baykal and takes you ultimately to Moscow.
Words or symbols on your computer screen
that can transport you instantly
to a curious or exotic site.
A single connecting element:
the caged-canary's riff, the scent of cedar,
the map that answers long-asked questions: how or where;
the letter hiding in a beat-up box;
the missing ancestor, who
more than any other, has given you
your breath, your song and story.

Metonymy's Economy

Along the block walls of the old foundation
her notes and diaries molder in deep boxes.
Outside, the sycamores drop rusty leaves.
We never think to ask who is in charge.

Her notes and diaries molder in deep boxes
close by the cradled cups of fine Limoges.
We never think to ask who is in charge,
what dust or destiny has kept a ledger.

Close by the cradled cups of fine Limoges
earwigs and mice are getting on quite well.
What dust or destiny has kept a ledger?
Who takes account: porcelain, paper, leather?

Earwigs and mice are getting on quite well
between the leaves of books, amidst the china.
Who takes account: porcelain, paper, leather?
Who cares to root in memory's scraps and shards?

Between the leaves of books, amidst the china
secrets still keep their marled and minted tales.
Who cares to root in memory's scraps and shards
will wish the vision keener in the dim illumination.

Secrets still keep their marled and minted tales.
No stains or scandals see the day's clear light
nor wish the vision keener in the dim illumination
along the block walls of the old foundation.

Our Turn

When we, as children, sat at Mother's table
and heard the talk that circled round the board—
which aunt had put up pears, and who was able
to can a mess of beans and still accord
some time to sewing for the Ladies' Aid,
which man had suffered illness, which one tossed
away his life just as his debts were paid—
these things we learned and scarcely knew our loss.
We passed the days and hoped that we might earn
the privilege of speaking out of turn.

We children asked the blessing for the meal
that kept us sitting up in straight-back chairs.
We must not squirm, or ask for a repeal
of clean-plate laws. Impertinent who dares
to challenge the decorum grown-ups need.
And so we pushed our peas around our plates,
not having, really, any case to plead,
and chewed on scraps of weather, haystacks, hates.
We passed the hours and thought that we would spurn
such niceties of discourse in our turn.

A Grave and Orderly Array

The coffin hoisted by six sturdy pall bearers
into the back of a waiting hearse, it disappears
and I hold back a sob. There'll be no burial.

Barbara is headed for the crematorium, where
all of what remains will soon become gray ash
contained within a lidded coffee tin

and given to next of kin. The indecorous urn
I place within my bedroom on the antique dresser.
It is an awkward part of the décor, incongruous

as the task that I keep putting off, resisting
its character. I'm seeking any form of grace
that might imbue the can of gritty residue—

of tooth and bone, toenail, and the tumor
crowding the space inside her body's rooms—
with dignity, as of a map of trails.

What does it mean to cast the ash upon the water?
From the littoral space return the desiccated cells
to their literal source, the sea? I live inland,

miles from any beach, yet so much closer
than our prairie kin to any ocean's waters.
The job has fallen to me

and to her little orphaned cat that I brought home,
who now jumps up to keep me company
where I lie weeping, dreading the ceremony.

At water's edge, with a stick I've brought,
I write her name in sand and watch the waves dissolve
its letters. It's like a signature of seaweed

the surf casts up and then sucks back again.
Years before, fixing our signatures
to Mother's death certificate, Barbara and I had tried

even in the surge of grief to muster a decorum
for the task of apportioning Mother's furniture—
those antique chairs (the ladder-back and Windsor),

the secretary, a dresser topped with marble,
a washstand and Victorian table. Yet still we fought
about the disposition of those pieces

through which she'd made her decorous claim
on selfhood—which ones we would claim as suited
to our own décor. I did not think to ask

the better question: Is there a decorum of the soul?
And if I could have staked a claim
on what then I scarcely could imagine,

I would have praised the toss and tangle the surf knows
in the reaches of its drawers and cubbyholes
and grace in names that let themselves be taken.

Yellow Water

The only way to get from there to here: snake through pipes
and scale the slippery banks of rivers. Do not slip.
The alligators—
they surface in yellow water.

Might I address myself to water lilies
and their capacious, floating leaves, and
skim across without much risk
to Barb in her pretty pajamas
expelling the last blood or Dad,
so seldom ill, napping on the couch
when he was taken? Or Mom
in a dawn-gray room surrounded by her bedrails?
Count them. Count the phone calls
surfacing in yellow water.

Not to have been there when they died
makes getting from there to here a little harder.
The corridors are crowded with clowns, car dealers,
clergy. I cannot navigate the yellow water.
And in the stairways and the vacant foyers
I hear echoes of my broken voice.
I stare at doors, names obliterated
from their small brass plates.
Was it just yesterday I knew them?

I wake,
the memories surface:
Mom at the sink peeling onions under running water,
Dad wrinkling his nose at a whiff of printer's ink
from the funny paper, Barb on the back porch,
spreading her toes to dry the polish.

Again the lily-padded pool. Step lightly, getting
from there to here. Again the phone, the voice, broken . . .

Count the alligators
surfacing in yellow water.

Siblings

> *for Barbara, 1942-1995*

i

Lost among shoppers' legs,
you dart into doorways.
The buckles on your sandals
glint as you disappear
around corners—a shadow child.

On the baked sidewalks of the courthouse square
I stay in the light at Mother's side.
Our shadows pool around our feet
and sunlight hums like bees
swarming in my light brown hair.

ii

Genuine rubber balloons are for sale
at Reeds Bookstore—a luxury during war.
Mother waits in line to buy her quota,
ties them, helium-filled, to our bedposts.

Years later, a photograph
of us at bedtime kneeling.
Now I lay me down to sleep
in one-piece, footed pj's.
If I should die before I wake
and the flap of my pajama bottom
droopy like Mother's coin purse,
while yours is taut
over your plump buttocks
like the skin of those rare balloons.

iii

You invite the neighborhood kids,
 "Come to my little school."
They come by twos and threes,
leaving their trikes and sandboxes
to sit in a circle of chairs.

Outside the halo of that play
I throw a tantrum when I learn
you've given away my favorite doll
to one your best scholars.

What if Mother could take back
the care she lavished on my misery,
apportion some of it to you
years later when, away at school,
you turned up pregnant?
There was no one then to say
"Come home to the circle of chairs,
O lovely one, and be our teacher."

iv

You stop the car and vomit in the bushes.
I vow to quell the words that start that poison drip,
speak only of the weather and our dead parents
as we drive out to shop for Christmas. Too warm,
this late fall day, too unseasonably mundane to be
our final family holiday. Silent in the car with us,
the brother we never had but wished for, silently.

Your presence hangs like dust motes
in the shafts of paler sun when next
I put my suitcase down in your guest bedroom.
Outdoors, tire tracks grooved in dirty snow
stop at the garage door still open on
your small black Mazda, hunched
like a frightened cat, waiting.

Ourselves, Afraid

It's hard not to notice the way
a funeral makes order
of the uncertainty of our lives.
How, emerging from our bedrooms
in best black dress or suit, we feel formal
and composed, as if contained
in picture frames. Like the dead,
today we make no decisions. We are encased
in custom, instructed where to sit, when to stand.
Our trumpets of individual style
are muted by decorum, and we are carried
on the long sea swell of words and music
as if we might continue to avoid
the vertiginous drop.
We know, and do not know
as bodies that in their internal resonance learn
the voices of a fugue.

Meadowlands

Meadows is its name—
cornfields abutting the highway into town,
grain elevator alongside the tracks.
Pastures skirt the outlying barns and sheds,
where cows may graze. An elder-care facility
runs its ramps down to the walks and well-cut lawns.
Each village house presides over its plot of grass.

In my dreamscape, Meadows isn't green—
not pastoral but proud, and hard with pavement.
Stone alleys, their sharp turns opening into
narrow courtyards, rough-hewn uneven steps
ascending to sun-baked terraces.
The only verdure is the weeds pushing through
crevices, hairy thistles sporting their purple flowers.

Clambering over cobbles, hugging the scant shade of walls,
I stop when suddenly given a small sun-powered car.
With this vehicle, I see a way
to gain the freeway, which, I'm told,
leads to the evergreen forest where, in a cool glade
families are feasting. But fortune here is meager . . .

Missing the turn to the access road—misconstruing
an avenue for the on-ramp, I'm routed into a maze of narrow,
rutted paths where every turn and twist takes me
farther from the torrid surfaces, deeper, to discover
a town's wet core. Here in its teeming cellar
I've no other course but to pay homage
to the savage greening of the meadowlands,
the non-negotiable energy rising from roots and stems.

Autumn Equinox

A field, an orchard, the still voice within.
Wind curls the dry leaf—a turning page.

The yield was light this year, the runted pippins,
parched alfalfa—loss too steep to gauge.

Unlock the piano; give the stool a spin.
Your work and tips won't make a living wage.

Bring in the groceries—chick peas, rice, and gin.
Begin to set the table, gathering the rage
of field and orchard, a father's voice grown thin:

*Next year, hire some Cubans, guys too dumb to win
in beisa-bol, or man the batter's cage.*

But now he's taciturn, subdued again.
The pastor's here for dinner, center stage.

Forget the field, the orchard, that still voice within.
You want to weep; instead you fake a grin.

She Told Me Stories

Grandma showed me how to turn
a neat hospital corner on a bed sheet.
Said that red fingernails were *not* what God intended,
else He'd have given me them. But she preened daily
at her glass, un-plaiting her silvery hair
and brushing, brushing it as if she were still
the belle of New Philadelphia pleased with her conquest,
a young widower with two tender boys, one of whom
one day would be my father.

Grown up, that boy to take a wife
and father children of his own.
He went to war, looted German warehouses
of silks and Turkish towels while we at home
flung our little bodies on the bed and cried out Daddy.
He bivouacked one night in a French town half bombed out,
awoke to find a woman cooking at her stove
and a small child playing on the floor
near the spot where he had shed his soldier gear
and claimed the right to sleep.

Grandma told her stories as if she were the family cat
regaling us of the hunt with birds laid upon the threshold—
tales of girls who rode in cars with boys.
She thought I barely listened, but I counted three:
one who married a professor,
one who crossed the sea,
and one who was pregnant and still in penny loafers.
Her voice crackled like syrup hardened in the snow.
I rubbed my class ring hard
and smoothed my pleated skirt.

History's Locomotive

after "Time Transfixed," by René Magritte

Imagine that engine bursting from the fireplace
on Christmas, carrying Mother's sweetheart,
Daddy, home on furlough. A grinding roar meets our awed hush
as, piercing the fireplace wall, it levitates above the hearth.
Maybe Mother remembers the troop train in Bloomington
that winter morning, carrying other women's husbands.
Maybe her mind plays tricks and she thinks only of the grate
Daddy had warned could send out sparks and set us all aflame.
We take that fire-driven thing into our midst—
so hot and yet so cold. It is Time's marker
in my parents' story. It opens
pauses in their sentences,
puts distance in their intimacy.

Before the fighting men spill to the platform,
she registers earth's tremor traveling under rails,
shoulders the locomotive's tonnage and houses
its oracular whistle—that increasing shrillness—
the penetration of its enlarging eye.
An auxiliary of wives and sweethearts waiting at the depot
with coffee and sandwiches for the troops
passing through on the GM&O. Mother has gone
without her headscarf, through the day is cold.
Her coat is buttoned over a cotton housedress,
but the seams of her stockings are straight.
Auxiliary means small glamour.

Does she thrill secretly to locomotive wheels,
connecter rods ramming and retracting, ribbon-curls
of steam? Does she imagine other engines crawling, hunkering,
their smoke stacks blossoming under terminals' glass domes—
Vienna, Brussels, Paris, Rome?

This is 1944—the gutted churches, charred and
smoldering houses, limbs and torsos sown in fields.
Here and there a station platform festive
with rumpled uniforms and kisses.

What is her dedication but an offering?
For Mother, raising toddlers without her helpmeet, it offers
the extravagance, maybe, of grand perspective—panoramas holding
sturdy locomotives trailing troop cars through
valleys and across plains under moon and clouds.

Modulations

Down in the church basement
women my mother's age
are rolling down their nylon hose,
peeling them over toes
and tucking each balled-up stocking
into a waiting shoe.
Feet white as bread or Gruyere cheese
beneath the crusts and rinds of calluses,
bunioned feet embossed with corns,
some rosy as trout
wiggling in the basin
submitting to another woman's hands,
the swathe of water, the caress

on this Palm Sunday morning when a rite
of Mennonites unfolds below the stairs
in even cadences of water poured from pitchers,
soles massaged in rough thin towels.
Lush chords in those G-major hymns
filter down from overhead, brimming,
settling toward their resolutions.

* * * *

Chords somersault and wrestle
in the broad stairwell while I descend
with Mother into Presser Hall's basement.
Her sturdy feet march me
through subterranean corridors
awash with the cacophony of rills and scales
to Miss Newcomb's studio

where she presides at a grand piano
administering corrections
or awarding stars. Soon I'll be
the kid on the bench, seeing her
raise a pair of glasses from her ample breast
shaking her jowls as she adjusts them.

For now, I have a brief reprieve
to wander, reading for the umpteenth time
quotations taped to the studio door
    We boil at different temperatures. —Emerson
(Mother avers Miss Newcomb is a Unitarian,
while outside in the fading light the feet of college students
pass at eye level.)
    The moon shown bright on Mrs. Porter
    And her daughter
    They washed their feet in soda water. —Eliot

    * * * *

Older, I go to lessons by myself,
taking the bus from school.
Leaving the studio at dusk
after an hour of scales and Bach,
the moon a tarnished token in my pocket,
I stand at the stop, legs raw in the wind,
feet stomping the blackened ice,
naming the makes of passing cars to Haydn's measures
and watching for the wide-spaced headlights of the bus.
Austere cadences are played on me,
my toes in stiffened shoes
so many piano keys.

Poem without the Piano

Even if you're expecting
just notes—
in tunes and rills
chords and counterpoint—
you may get minnows silvered
darting in little schools
or sumo wrestlers panting
groaning with the contest.
You may get Chinese acrobats
stacked up in pyramids
or paddle balls
or yo-yos
whirligigs
Pick-up-Stix
painted turtles
crawling from fissures
between the keys. Things
whose happening
takes shape in spaces
between the sounds.

Thirteen

Karen and I jumped the ditch water
near a fenced-in pasture
that dwindled out into a smudgy sunset.
Soon there'd be cake and mattresses,
six girls giggling through ghost stories
and someone who had cramps.
It wasn't our bravado scattering hens
or even stealing their warm, straw-stippled eggs.
It was the riding bareback on a swaybacked mare,
the ache in the crotch,
and Karen's older brother stalking us
from bushes in the humid dark.

Playing Outside

The grade-school playground:
a lot done
with steel pipes,
with elbow joints & t's,
socketed joints like v's—
the framework for swings
that hung from creaking, clanking
chains. The monkey bars,
their horizontals polished
to a dull patina by
the undersides of knees,
the jungle gym, its stern
geometry.

Fat, aluminum-painted pipe
with feet cemented in the ground
made the fulcrum for the teeter-
totter's bleached gray boards
grown splinter-y in the sun.
Precarious to mount the see-saw
when, at opposite ends,
you & your playmate
leveled the board
& throwing one leg over,
eased your buttocks down.
No handles there to grasp,
only the fist-sized indentations cut
into the board's sides.

It took some kind of nerve
when forward-pitched
at 45 degrees
you looked
your playmate in the eye,
tried not to grimace
when your body bounced,
lifting your rear end off the board
as his end hit the gravel.
It took a timing fine
as any surfer's
to settle back a little sooner,

shifting your weight to lift him
to the balance point
& past, gaining
the momentum of the fall,
then absorbing it into your legs,
your knees
to soften the tooth-jarring jolt
of your end's touching.

You took that work
for play, you & he.
Came racing back
for more,
hollering.

To a Washing Machine

Brash and naked,
you stand shameless
in your newness
inside the block walls
of the old foundation
behind
the furnace,
between
a rust-stained sink
and a drain hole
in the floor.
Monday mornings
Mother leaves
the kitchen's warmth and light,
descends the narrow
stairs,
bearing offerings
of underwear and aprons,
towels
bed sheets,
tablecloths.
Unlike the furnace,
that hearty old trunk
that sends its air ducts
branching across
the ceiling,
you have just one
bold flower,
a wringer.
Stiff and serviceable,
it looks more sinister
than song inducing.
We children circle
the basement

on our skates
while Mother
feeds the wringer's maw.
We hear
the suck of water,
thump
of the dowel
with which she stuffs
the wringer's lips.
Watch it gobble up
each juicy bit
she offers
then swivel
forty-five degrees
to repeat the sequence
over tubs of rinse.
There's never any question
who's in charge.
And not until
it's time
to shake out sheets
do we find usefulness
in this routine.
We hold
the edges
while our mother
clasps the wooden pins
between her teeth,
raises one corner
to the line
and then
the heavy middle
then the end.
How we love to skate

through humid
corridors
between the lines
of sheets
then burst out,
flapping wings!

Winter's Tales

for Janet

i

I think I've talked about our crow, the one
who'd often come to drink beside the curb,
who'd dip his beak and sip, sweet as a priest
from pools the leaky sprinkler head had made.

Worked up a bit of a routine, that crow:
jump in and splash, look up, step off the curb
and strut about on 10th. His plumage jet
and almost lacquered in the sun. What rite

or trading of a glance could make us see
as one? No dance so jaunty as his hop
nor garb so formal as his furled wing.
His look, intelligent, would make me ask,
So? Crow.

ii

Now I must tell you of our rat. That rogue
field fellow found us out some way, set up
his place beneath a cupboard, through a hole,
then issued forth to make our house his own.

Small rat he was to trail a tail so long.
The cats, though riveted at first, grew bored.
They thought, I guess, he'd earned asylum like
our bird. Assumed we'd welcomed him to be

our rat. He balanced on the curtain rod
and twitched his parchment ears; he fixed me with
obsidian gaze; I quailed. *He likes you,* was
my friend's response. Ambivalent, I thought,
Ciao! Rat.

To My Singing Partner

Dear Howie, you were very sweet to mail
your song. Last Tuesday when you phoned to ask
if I would write some lyrics for it—hell,
I thought, why not? Wouldn't take me to task
for anything I wrote, you promised—smog
or tail pipes, hats with flowers. Just let it flow,
my feelings, from the heart! My friend, our dialog
(let's cut the hooey) has not been pure as snow
for all the old-time hymns we sing in duo
week in, week out, at Rose's piano.
I need thee every hour... Enticements hide
beneath our sallies and retorts. "You're fired,"
I threaten. Then you press a hand, shyly expressive,
against my back as we are singing. Blessing.

Birdsong

I cannot call it mirth, so I'll say yellow
for the way it slathers butter on my toast, tops
my tumbler with a lemon slice, proffers mellow
lute-bellied squash, the best of autumn's crop.

Dandelion wild, it stirs the curtain's column,
thrusts branches of forsythia across the sill
in wands to rarify my dreams with saffron,
amber, gold, a sorcerer's daffodil.

For arias, a warbler's repertoire—
dispatch of wayward lifts, like taxi cabs
that carry me to places heretofore
unknown, where every syllable's up for grabs.

This half-drunk courier between earth and sky,
like a zigzag bee stopped at The Daisy's Eye.

II

*. . . some branches always spin toward the trunk of the tree,
a motion lost in the stuttering of leaves.*
—Brent Armendinger

Tree Men

An aging Boomer whose beard is trimmed
in 'nineties style, my tree man strolls across
the porch and rings the bell. We greet and nod
acknowledgment. "Let's go around back," I say.
"Several of our fruit trees need attention."

Phil sees the stumps of hacked-off limbs, regrets
the insouciance of earlier pruners, shows
where trunk rot has set in, the consequence
of branches not cut cleanly at their joints.
He kneels at the apricot's base, he thumbs a lesion:
"You've got a borer beetle here," then points
to a carbuncle of sap that shows the tree
at work expelling it. Loquat and fig,
peach—they all need greatly trimming back.
"Take out the plum. It's rotten to the core."

"Come see the avocado," then he warns.
"Those vines of creeping fig will choke its life
if they continue spreading up the trunk
along each branch." He stops to heave a sigh.
I nod. On his canary-yellow pad
he notes how much each portion of the job
will cost. At his departure I peruse
the list. I gulp. Then I decide to get
another tree man's estimate next day.

The wife sounds grumpy on the phone that night,
not well attuned, as Mack turns out to be.
Unfastening the gate, I watch him bound
into the yard—a terrier loosed from leash.
I point to loquat and prodigious fig,
to struggling peach and spreading apricot.
He blinks and shrugs. "You wouldn't lose too much
by taking out these trees and starting new."

Then seeing my indignation and chagrin,
"But maybe you want to go with what you've got."
I give him points for savvy. Then I move
toward the avocado's viney trunk.
"What would you do with this? (I hear myself)
I'm scared to death the creeping vine will kill it."

His answer takes me wholly off my guard:
"A tree, it likes to have its bark protected.
Y'r avocado, it's especially prone
to sunburn."
        Then he moves into his spiel:
"Your trees want different things than folks, you see.
Trees like to have low branches to protect
their bark—that's like a skin—from too much sun.
They like to wallow in deep beds of leaves
up to their ankles, to keep moisture in.
Here by your deck, mankind has had his way:
he's pruned protecting branches back and back,
exposing nude and tender bark these vines
have risen to protect. Remove them now,
you'll doubtless kill the tree." He jots his price
upon a card. Then briskly through the gate
he's gone before I get the chance to say
another word.
        I'm left to muse and ponder
how it would be if I left town for good—
left trees to fare as well as fare they could
without my interference. Would they grow
lush skirts and thrive? Or would they lose the fight
against the borer beetle, scorch and blight?

You, there

leaning 45 degrees to the ground,
limbs all sprawl-y out, randomly up,
as if to right yourself. All odd
curves and trajectories, they writhe
like a nest of snakes. Winter,
when you're naked, I'll do my surgery.
Arms and fingers—scores of amputations—
until you're shapely and contained,
a work of sculpture, almost beautiful.
For six weeks or a month, that is.
End of February, your sap begins
to rise. Don't think I don't notice
those brand new fingers you flaunt
at the ends of your stumpy arms
and your manicure of Easter green.
Almost before I can say *lettuce*
or *lapin,* those jelly beans open
into Sunday handkerchiefs, spread out
to dinner plates, and finally assume
the dark-green, leathery mien
of welders' aprons (no wonder
Eve and Adam found them handy).
Fruit? Oh my, yes. At first
you're rather modest,
half hiding them like firm, pink
earlobes under heavy tresses.
But you can't keep it that way,
can you? Come July and August
your offerings are more like fulsome nipples,
rippled skin the color of brothel-curtain velvet.
Gnats, flies and bees dart
in and mosey out. Mornings
there's evidence of rats' nocturnal
romps. Your smooth jewels

open like geodes to reveal crystals
delectable to the mouth—if insects
have not invaded from a split in the skin
to feed now from within. By September
I would be quit of you,
My Nemesis, My Mess. I would
cut you down, dry out your limbs
to use as kindling, but that you stubbornly
persist, insisting on your right to be.

Elsewhere

A Bouts Rimés Sonnet

Powerful lot of nerve it takes: she flees
the agents with celebs in tow, that zone
of meretricious kisses, sexy knees.
Offstage at last to meet her ghost alone!
Oh there'll be questions, then the offerings
of cassoulet and ripened brie. *You slave,*
the kettle murmurs, and Madonna sings.
Tomorrow she'll be jocund; she'll engrave
initials on the fairy tree, or guess
the words to mockingbirds' libretti. Cog
the wheel, perhaps, call up the hostess
for self-exiled hermits who would slog
through this epiphany leaving thumb
prints on the tumblers, glugging shots of rum.

I, Voyeur

>   *after Jan Vermeer, "Young Woman Seated at a Virginal"*

His gaze is toward the dark recesses
of the room where in the foreground a girl
turns from her music, as if waiting for a cue,
caught in the half-second when

her fingertips touch the keyboard.
Her arms catch sunlight from a source
outside the picture's frame. It seems
Vermeer's decided that he'll place

his customary window where the shadows
gather, leaving it shuttered so that
light must enter through a fourth-wall,
past a swag of drapery

and an upright cello, bright
like a huge, sun-burnished leaf. From light,
I draw toward the darkened center, where my path
meets the painter's in that peculiar space

between the oval of the young girl's head
and billowing under-sleeve. I slip
across her neck and shoulder on a string of pearls,
take refuge in a background less intense

defining the curve of back and shoulder.
Behind the young musician at the instrument, a picture
hangs—*The Procuress* of Dirck van Baburen,
a scene where money changes hands, transaction

shrewd and venal. I see the picture frame,
gilt-wrought around the canvas on the wall
and the yards of azure silk festooning from
the sitter's waist, mounding behind her

on the chair. And in the background,
tiles along the floor, those Delft miniatures
I suppose depict quotidian transactions:
wives churning butter or turning spitted pigs,

men haggling in the market, riding with the hunt.
archers shooting arrows, peddlers sharpening knives.
The scenes appear in my imagination, no sooner
formed than they dissolve again. This girl, though,

she attends. She looks me in the eye as if
I could but nod and she would start to play—
play her subjectivity into this room, her world,
not knowing that already it's been bartered.

The Comtesse d'Haussonville with *Nature Morte*

*after Jean-Auguste-Dominique Ingres,
"Comtesse d'Haussonville"*

She leans, composed, against the mantle's edge
of a small upholstered fireplace sheathed in velvet.
She lets the light, hot and still in the summer room, blanche
those rotund arms and steal from them their contours.

She need not bless herself. Her gown is yards of silk
cascading from her waist to frothy flounce
of ruffle, ruched sleeves caught up with floppy bows.
She's warm but would not think of seeming so. Her dress
speaks calmly of the hues of cloudless sky that soon
enough will deepen into evening's shadow.

Already dusk has brushed her mirrored nape,
composing a still-life with the tawny melon-wedge
of upper back and shoulders, the oriental basket
of her braided, coiled hair held by a tortoiseshell comb.
Blossoms of spendthrift rose and slender tulip
in cache-pots on the mantle seem the more replete
for being doubled in their reflection in the mirror.

A ribbon, scarlet as a rooster's comb,
rides aside the coil of braid, its prominent rosette
descending into swags of graduated loops.
In that *nature morte* seen behind her in the mirror,
this opulence could be the crimson skins of peppers
or the gash that scores the rabbit's throat.

Jane Carlyle Laments

> *... she felt like an animate suitcase with his name on it.*
> *Phyllis Rose, "Parallel Lives"*

My suitcase emptied hours ago, I want an occupation.
In the wardrobe, my few dresses, except the one
laid out to wear to dinner. A whiff of lavender . . .
I was fond once of this ivory cameo,
memento of another life when I was just a girl—
witty, companionable, and counting the months
between Mr. Carlyle's letters.

Clever I believe I was. Father used to urge me,
"Write, Lass." And I delighted in it. I took him my novel
and the next year brought my five-act tragedy to his discerning eye.
At home in Haddington nothing pleased him more.
"All Scotland shall know of Jane Baillie Welsh!"

Mother reveled in other prospects, counting the suitors
for their heiress. Even after Poppa died, I flourished
as fire thrives on air. Some said I was flirtatious.
And yes, I ignited sparks and shook some embers
while I awaited letters from that Mr. Carlyle.

Not I, but Thomas now—Mr. Carlyle, the cynosure
of gazes. He displays his ebony intellect, polished
to a gloss for Lady Ashburton and her coterie. Let him!
Let these stagnant days, these sterile nights be my reward
for shushing a rooster's cock-a-doodle-do—my diplomacy
with our neighbor who kept backyard hens.
And my husband's raging in the dawn, stomping.
I shuddered in my bed.

I admire a rooster as much as I despise forbearing hens,
but Thomas must have his sleep. I based my argument
on Mr. Carlyle's weighty contribution to the world
and got that woman to shut the rooster up inside the house
while Thomas and I enjoyed a brief reprieve, buttering our toast,
inhaling the fragrance of our morning tea. Yet still it seemed
that Thomas could not work. Trains shook the house,
their whistles screaming. Vendors squawked and yodeled.
The soundproof room we built upstairs—a sham.

Now there's the bell: we're summoned
to Harriet Ahsburton's drawing room for sherry.
What do I want with cordials? Jane is not Jane
without her words. Could I but puff my chest
and crow a little! Let Thomas read and scribble
in the radiance of Lady Ashburton's smile.
I shall pen my thoughts in this dim light.

Letters to Ralph Waldo Emerson from His Second Wife

> *Over his active career of four decades, Emerson gave some 1,500 public lectures.*
> Robert D. Richardon, Jr., Emerson: The Mind on Fire

23 February, 18—

I snatch an hour to write, dear Husband,
regretting that so poor and hasty and epistle
must reach your eyes. I mean to amend my ways.
Your son Eddy crows beneath the table,
making sentries of clothespins,
a tower of measuring cups.
From the comfort of my lap,
our Edith helps me write.

Henry entertained us yesterday
with bird calls rendered on his flute,
transforming our parlor into a forest glen.
He promises a letter in this packet.

Last night's snow weighs down
the fir tree branches, glorious with their burden!
I dreamt then of meeting Ellen when you and I
had gone to heaven. I could do naught but go away,
leaving you with her.
Waldo, I covet the deep bell
of your voice from the study, yet I cannot
begrudge the words you tender others
from the podium.

I sign myself Lidian,
your affectionate Wife,
and mother of your children.

2 June, 18—

To catch time on the wing
I put my pen to paper. Even so,
your weeks at home fly by more swiftly
than each hour that you are absent.

Our dear Elizabeth arrived this morning,
pleasing Mother with new lettuce
and a jar of berry conserve.
Our Edith often halts her play to fetch
her grandma's ball of wool or thimble.
This afternoon she stopped to wash her face
before presenting herself at dinner!

Waldo, dearest Friend, if only you could
see the children daily, I think you would approve
their God-given wisdom.
Ellen chided me this morning
when I complained that I should die
if she would not stop fretting:
"No Mother, you will not."
I blush reporting this.

Your favorite plum tree's set with fruit,
not numerous but promising . . .

I tender my devotion as
your Wife,
      Lidian
        (your second wife,
          the mother of your children)

Hymn Meters, after Emily

i

It crystallized in granite wheels—
A gravel on the walk.
It dropped a tuft of feathers down
To pave the way for talk.

We were oppressed with knowing then
The sunlight and the gleam
Of harder diamonds than can come
From screws on carbon's frame.

ii

Temper your knives with emery—
Bury your quills in silk.
Post letters written yesterday—
Sealed with the opal's milk.

Spangle the pinecones on the sill
With desiccated snow—
Whistle a song sealed in the June
That red-winged warblers know.

iii

A tight epistle—penning it—
A sonnet rich in rage—
Each fiery glyph a predicate
For time's replete mirage.

Constraint would be a molten sea
Within St. Helen's dome—
Without the shift that tips release—
And lava's viscous tome.

III

If names and trees and sky, if field and skin and story could be distilled into an essence of the used heart . . .

We Are Occasional Like That

>   *after reading Jack Gilbert's "Refusing Heaven"*

We don't add up the way our birthdays do,
nor are we merely calendar pages
torn off, discarded one by one. We're not the sum of our experiences.
More like the weather that may blur the seasons
but gives each day its edge.

We are not the swing any more than the branch that holds it.
More like the energy in pumping legs, the arc described in the air

or resonance that lingers when the bells' polyphony
has ceased, the elated silence when the *angelus* subsides.

We are occasional like that. Like those times as lovers when
we chance to close the distance separating every living being
from the object of its love. The moment when *each* gives way
to *both* and we live neither in the camera nor the snapshot
but in the instant when wings flap

and a bird takes flight, unaware
of its trailing feet.

Benton's Hailstorm

after "the picture" by Thomas Hart Benton

Raptured
in that instant when
lighting forks down
and stumps and grasses blanch
with phosphorescence—
have I not wished it?
It's heaven and hell at once:
familiarity subverted in undersea forms
of undulating leaves and octopus stumps,
the air grown sulfurous and heavy,
the great rocks porous, spongy.
It's the mayhem that I crave—
wind so strong the very world bends
and man and beast are bent on finding
shelter, even while
yearning to be taken.

Benton's mule charges toward the shed.
Wind-driven thunderheads charge
the pearly resident sky
like purple-green forebodings
humping their backs and hissing
fire. The gnarled tree's turned bestial
in collusion, flinging leaves like flames
from the mouths of its tossing boughs.
Heaven's on the horizon,
if only I could get there
across the field's rich corduroy furrows
straining toward the light
bowed in darkness.

Towards Evening, Overcast

Inverted green foliage,
sky's flannel gray hue—
this pond is a mirror.
What more can I do

when glimpsing my face
in its specular view
than admit myself double,
both wanton and true.

Falling Asleep

The center of the palm,
foot's arch and small of back,
places that do not ordinarily
serve as points of contact
with the ground—how is it that
when on the verge of sleep
sometimes I'm aware
of these small
sheltered grottoes
under vaults of bone
and feel that I own them?
Even the space that floats
between my outstretched fingers,
or glances off my forehead
like the loopy lines and folds
transfiguring themselves
on a computer's screen.

As I lie still, the bed sheets
warm around me.
The edges of my body melt, until
it fills the heated envelope, a candle nub,
still burning, subsiding
into a saucer-shaped pool of wax.
Then I extend a leg,
reclaiming its contours
in the tingle of chilly percale.

Clods are prodding my instep arch.
I'm gathering cabbages
or dusting the wormy ones
with a tumbled compound
of slaked lime and sifted ash.
Fields are fanning out, brown
in the slanting light behind

my speeding form.
Acres of goldenrod and wild carrot
tumble with fuchsia sky
as end over end
I roll like a giant weed
toward the dark horizon.

Ceremony

for two married at the Candlelight Wedding Chapel, Reno

A peal of laughter underneath the stair,
the floating petals where their voices dropped,
and always the style, the spin, that certain flair.

Beneath the fog, the early chefs prepare
buffet, while lovers whinny as if sleep had cropped
a peal of laughter underneath the stair.

Twin candelabras' pristine wicks declare
that flames cost extra. Still they can adopt
the city's glitz, its style, that certain spin and flair.

The driver earns no salary: peevish wear
and tear on nuptial glee, which roguishly concocts
a peal of laughter underneath the stair.

For baking, body building, bicycle repair
she puts away her fashionable sequined tops.
But always the style, the spin, that certain flair.

They live the lives of lovers sipping air
or smoothies, lounge on pillows propped.
A peal of laughter underneath the stair
and always the style, the spin, that certain flair.

Urbane Pianos

Snatch of music from a passing car—
cool jazzy piano in a New Orleans bar.

Honky-tonk piano in a Harlem dive,
Amsterdam Avenue at 1:25.

Lacquered piano shines like it's wet
and the Vegas blond who sings this set

hugs its curve and shows some sass,
but the keyboard guy is devoid of class.

The concert piano in a London hall
awaits the musician, tuxedoed but small.

Its top is open, an elegant valve.
Who cares if the pianist is only twelve?

Powder-blue piano in a Chelsea loft:
ballet-school workhorse yields no soft

tones from its hammers and strings
grown tired from countless accompanyings.

Furry piano in a St. Petersburg square:
you'll need fingerless gloves to play it there.

Its keys are icy, its sound displaced,
despite its gorgeous otter case.

Its grandeur belies its diminished powers.
The gig's played out, both the piano's and ours.

Trimaran

Sailing the sea in a three-hulled boat, I thrilled
(as who would not) to look behind me
at the trimaran's course—a vanishing issue
of triple wakes, furrows inscribing the plain.

I stood solitary aboard one outer hull, shielding
my eyes against the glare, knowing in my gut
the captain expected me to swim
to the central craft and board it—
a courier whose journey was the message.

The route, seen bird-like from above, was elegant,
the distance measured by a wing beat. But from
the gunwale where I stood, an abyss between
me and the haven of that other hull's embrace.

I could see the start, the finish: knife plunge through
the glassy surface, and my spent body pulled up
—ropes and hands.

I Experience Agriculture

I. On the Detasseling Crew

A Latinate compound's too abstract
for what it's really like
swimming in high corn.
Green corridors,
tentacles of coarse leaves'
casual, rude caress.
I reached
with tired arms
up to the tassel—
platinum sparkler in shimmering blue.
The grasp,
the yank,
and then the rain—
just a sprinkle—of golden atoms
settling at the neckline,
on the sleeve.

II. In the Packing Shed

Even less visible
the fuzz of field-ripe peaches.
Crate after crate,
I pulled them off
the conveyor belt
and sorted them,
by hand as much as sight,
palm and fingers
assessing rotundity
and weight.
At night, the itching:
rising from wrists to fold of elbow,

along the tender inner arm,
levered into armpit,
where a rash breaks out.
The body rebuffs such intimacy—
this surfeit of velvet.

III. In the Abstract

To such luxury
I owe my sensate knowledge
of their industry—the leaf,
the stalk, the tassel and the fruit.
I didn't need the job
like Rose or Darla did
who worked the row beside me
or the bay ahead.
For me, the pay was spending money
I could take
and walk away.
I stashed my wages in between
lined notebook pages,
where no one but me
could hear them murmur
ager, agrestis, agricola,
agricultor, agricultura.

Quince

Across the north-south artery empty at this hour
except for the early car whose headlights cleave
the fog, I make my way

into the next subdivision. I'm looking for quince—
on the little tree whose owner said
to come and pick as soon as they are ripe.

Furred and bulbous, the fruit show gray-green
in the street light's milky halo,
fat purses loading the tree beside the walk.

Decibel by decibel, they ripen, absorbing
the freeway traffic's din, the grumble and chirp
of the Laidlaw bus as it brakes

before the assisted-living house to load passengers
and, heavy with indifference, carry them,
stifled, to the adult day-care center.

Cydonia oblonga, this *pomme* of ancient heritage,
ur-apple, primitive pear that's
ampler in circumference than it is long—

"The fuzzy quince originating in
the middle and near East," where they
may fatten, for all I know, on rounds of mortar fire

in Basra's stricken orchards, Baghdad's gardens
until Iraqi women and their kids harvest
all that remain and cook them

with scarce honey, into preserves. Or strain
the fragrant, woody pulp to make a nectar supersaturated,
heavy. History's ration, their cordial of gain and loss.

Borrowed Landscape

Here at Entsu-ji
A garden of stones and trees
Frames a strong mountain.
The mossy rocks seem fractals
Of Hiei-san's dark face.

Moss-covered or bare,
Each stone of this stern garden
Makes its own landscape.
I could be a small creature
At its base, awestruck, wanting.

Shadows play upon
Hiei-san's brow as clouds sweep
Across the sun's path.
What way is free from sorrow,
What life from disappointment?

Bending Water

> *At Kyoto's Kamigamo Shrine a legend recalls a custom of the 9th-10th centuries, when the Kyoyusui-en were held. These parties along the banks of the "bending water" featured a ceramic bird on which a cup of sake floated. While waiting for the cup, the ladies and gentlemen were required to compose poems.*

Swift runnels move
Deftly, strong and clear, singing.
My pen too must sing
So that my poem will welcome
Floating bird, cup of sake.

Flowering branches,
Light refracted in water.
I kneel on the bank.
O that I might catch the eye
Of the man to whom I write.

The season changes.
Spring pulses into summer.
Sun spangles water.
In this limpid watercourse,
Daily now I cleanse myself.

Ginseng on Court Street

in memory of Josephine D'Esposito, 1927-2004

I. Disproportion

Respite from being useful was
what mattered to me then amidst
the disproportion of a family Christmas
in the homes of my grown-up children—
clearing the breakfast table,
pouring their cups of tea.

I found it sauntering the Brooklyn streets
in Carroll Gardens: Court Street shops
of tailors, bakers, stationers, and sellers
of used dishes—those old Italians ready to chat
or cheat me when I poked in to nose around.

II. Josie Pours Half-and-Half

Ancient athletic pants and a worn fleece pullover,
two white braids dangling beside her ears from the plush
of a red velveteen cap—I wanted her to be
Mrs. Claus in Brooklyn. She nailed me for a stranger
as I crossed her threshold. "Josie Java," she hollered,
"Gotta pee." And she left me standing amidst the tinsel,
colored lights, the small unhopeful Santas dressed in dingy velvet.
I found a place to sit at one of the mismatched tables.

Josie presided from her counter perch
and barked my order to her cook, got up
to serve my eggs and bacon on a paper plate.
Her only grace was whitening my *cauffee*.
"Say when." And then she wheeled around,
reclaimed her right to gossip with the regulars,
relished some news of the day: a Chinese woman mugged.
"They went into her boobs for it," Josie howled.

III. Demography

Once it would have been an Irish Christmas.
For some time, though, the Caputos and Friellos, the Raccuglias
and the Leones have set the tone in Carroll Gardens.
Josie's Java held its place on Court Street in the block between
Frank Caputo's cheese shop and St. Mary Star of the Sea.

Last June, inside a letter from my daughter
a tribute clipped from the New York Times
to Josie and her place. For us, that dim establishment a novelty:
neither of us had been there more than once.

Imagine, then, Memorial Day, the grate down
before the door of Josie's shop and mass being said for her,
dead of a heart attack at 76. Dead after pouring countless cups,
dead after calling me *Sweetheart*. After adding the price
of the daily paper to my tab and squabbling with the
customer who brought his own to read while sipping.

IV. A Sense of Place

"I'll miss her, yelling over there," said Andy Cho,
businessman, from his health-food emporium
across the street from Josie's Java. Maybe Mr. Cho
stopped in at Josie's wake, placing a pot of white chrysanthemums
beside the gaudy sprays of long-stemmed gladiolas,
murmuring condolences with eyes lowered to the shoes
of Josie's four grown sons. Maybe.

It's Josie's moxie that I'm thinking of.
That raw December day, the lights of Christmas winking
and her harsh notes sounding, already of the past:
a moment distant enough for two strangers to meet,
reluctant hostess, nosey guest. I had stepped into her place
to forget whatever it was that kept us pouring.

In Eisenstadt, Visiting the Jewish Museum

i

A merchant-rabbi owned the ghetto's biggest house. Today
I'm walking through its rooms—traveler touring a museum.

"Our windows looked towards the towers of the Esterhazy Palace,"
one of his tenants said. This year beneath the palace towers

I rehearse a Mass that Joseph Haydn wrote as resident composer
for the House of Esterhazy. If when I'm backstage

with singers, cellists, masters of tympani and horn, I notice
on the wall a coat peg tagged with a nameplate, *Haydn*,

am I not thrilled to sing my part? Am I not part
of history, my story interleaved with chronicles of patronage,

with calendars of festival, and seasons of siege
and persecution? I've paid in Euros for my entry.

ii

To settle, put one's print upon the land, hold a house.

191 households in 1836: 378 rooms of folk

food cooked in 154 kitchens

provisions safe in 16 storerooms.

Room to room to room, houses held
quotidian striving interspersed with rest.

Is history this daily round
or is it catastrophe and stop?

iii

Museum walls, their documents and photos. Is history
the house itself—its thresholds, murmuring floorboards?
Goblets on the table set for *Seder,* and at one place a plastic cup
with ears. Cutlery and china, and Father's pillow on his chair.

A suite of armchairs with settee around a parlor table.
On *Shabbat* no one stirred a pot or dusted furniture.

A model *schule,* faint ghosts of scratching pens
on copybooks leant up against the slanted backs of seats ahead.
Sunlight shafting through large windows.

And then a room entirely painted black,
its only feature a white banner stretched from wall to wall,
simulation of one hung across a street in Eisenstadt:
Juden unerwünsncht – "Jews not wanted."

These staunch denizens, dependable, dependant—
their days (some days) were benedictions
not unlike mine as I sink into an upholstered chair
at the Schloss Café on the far boundary of Jerusalem Platz.

Prince Paul Esterhazy wrote in 1690 a *letter of safe conduct.*
Today the walls of the synagogue surrender names of the dead.

Without a Holocaust Room, there would be no museum. It follows
there would be no poem without the shadow of a holocaust.

iv

These storied rooms:
to pass through, speaking,
when I dare, in quiet cadences
while inside my head spaces ring
with covenants, songs, and prayers.

I cannot add my voice to voices
rebounding from these walls and panes
(as much as that would ease me)
or blend my footfalls with percussion
from these old planks and stones.
My history, another house.

Proving Ground

i

Under the lights of the high school gym
I curl like an infant. Just hours earlier
my body had belonged to history—
a frieze of warriors doubled by our shadows.

I've surrendered my shoes, my belt, my wallet.
Even the handcuffs, gone. Sheriff's deputies
had hauled us in sun visors and t-shirts stenciled
with the peace-sign across the desert
to Tonopah and this gymnasium, our holding tank.

Those handcuffs were nothing but a plastic band.
My arms hung from my shoulders,
the pendulum of a stopped clock.

ii

In the morning glare I'd made my footprint
in the dust of Federal ground. No sign
of the emplacement towers that lower bombs
into the earth, craters that pock-mark its skin.

Ahead of me, a Paiute chieftain paused midway
and raised a piece of paper, his words like spring water
gushing from fissures, giving back the land
its ancient rows and furrows—melon vines and squash,
corn and glancing sunflowers. Memory's deep seed.

iii

Who remembers when *Alamogordo* and *Trinity* were household words? Still wonders at the extravagant beauty of the Cloud?

Who remembers duck and cover?

Who is a down-winder from St. George or Cedar City?

Who buried mothers, uncles, aunts, cousins, kids or fathers dead of
    cancer?

Whose kids come home from school with tales of Yucca Mountain
    Johnny?

Whose is the luxury: not knowing?

iv

To walk a mile under candid sky to prove myself
against an artifice of power. To step across a line

I'd pulled on loose white pants and an old white shirt
guarding against the sun. I wanted to be baptized
in a sudden desert storm, my drenched skin shining
through transparent cloth—
                      a bell washed clean,
                                  ringing.

For a Woman Washing Vases

Having early found inside her chest an empty place,
she knows to fill with zest each empty space.

As a kid, she wanted to be pushed "higher, higher!"
In the arc of the backyard swing, she'd test the empty space.

While camping in the desert, she lets her dormant muscles
warm with the rising sun. Stretching is best in empty space.

An isolated butte, outcrop of rock above the level plain
lures her upward to its crest—an empty space.

Even the streets of her home city offer grist.
The pigeon builds her nest in an empty space.

Vines cling to walls, weeds shoot through cracks,
the vagrant man finds rest in an empty space.

At home she gently washes vases stained by decaying stems
as if to cherish wholeness, not molest the empty space.

This writer, whose name means *light,* invokes the source
of radiance, that words may fleetingly invest an empty space.

Instructions for the Lucia-let

The poem must use three lights:

    Avoid the moon and stars, if possible,
    the lighthouse beam, the firefly.
    Avoid the lighted clock-face in a tower.

    Incorporate the bathroom night light
        or a glowing cigarette, for instance;
            a miner's lamp, a Bunsen burner.

    These lights must end the first lines of the poem's three
        stanzas.

Weave in an allusion to Italian opera
    or to a martyred saint, her eyes poked out,
        or to a girl with candles in her crown.

Include a reference to the scientific method
    or to a famous experiment of science.

The poem must enact conflict and embody strife
    but not entirely avoid a closure.

    Light must go to bed with darkness, roll around with it,
        tangle in its embrace. It must be pierced and
            shattered, scatter and all-but-disperse. . .
    (do not try to avoid
    the masculine/feminine allusion—
    spark and tinder of the human quarrel).

The point is for the poem to come to resolution
    not naked but still clinging to a scrap of clothing. It must

collapse into a chaos, then, of order
like the lightless tank from which occasionally
      a neutrino traveling incognito from the sun
          is intercepted
                with a little   flash.

Roller Skating with Walt Whitman

Just think how much more of Manhattan
You could see, Walt!
Come. Don this pair of skates.
Strap these wheels to your feet.
Let the roughness of the pavement vibrate through your bones.
Let the push of your legs and the swing of your arms propel you.
Let your gaze be far and near,
Seeing the skyscrapers and sidewalk cracks,
Seeing the sunset reflected in many windows
And the dapper missionaries with their tracts.
Seeing the grand marquees and the Good Humor men,
And the beggars in their patient bodies,
And the noble statuary, and pigeons strutting in the squares.
Seeing stylish women with their handbags
And plain women pulling carts.
Put your skates on, Walt,
And follow me.
Or if you lead, I will follow,
Whirling with you in the ranks of multitudes,
Finding myself in the streamers of your hatband
Flying in the wind.

Found Horses

I. Equine Skeleton, Mount Holyoke College

Not dry, these bones, marrowed with ancient earth,
its grasses and the milk of its grains
parlayed to muscle and tendon fallen away now.
Blood still seems to fire the flesh of flanks
rippling under a chestnut coat;
to quicken the neck and withers.

This horse in the basement corridor of Clapp Laboratory
was Cynthia Willard's project. Box upon box
of bones, like calcified twigs and branches,
she numbered them, fit the knobs into their sockets
like puzzle pieces, notched together breast-bone
armature and skull helmet. Assembled, they repel
the dusk of a shadowed hallway—ghost horse
remembering the meadow.

II. Equine Statue, Minneapolis Sculpture Garden

Found-wood found itself becoming bone and sinew
as Deborah Butterfield built her horse of tree bark,
branches, cast-off boards and sticks,
their grain raised by wind-blown rain and grit.
Muscle and lineament, one at a time she made molds conform
to each branchy, wooden element, and into these
she poured a molten metal that burnt away the core.
The bronze bones cooled.
                    She built them up, new minted,

into hoof and hindquarters, muzzle, tail, and hank of mane.
She gave them the patina of weathered wood.
Thus Woodrow was born
to claim his place under the trees, along the grass-edged path—
trick horse, inhabiting both the figure and the ground.

Notes

The title of the poem "Venus and Other Losses" was suggested by Maureen Alsop.

"Letters to Ralph Waldo Emerson from His Second Wife" contains references to Henry David Thoreau (1817-1862), a good friend of the Emersons; to Ellen Tucker, Emerson's wife from 1829 until her death in 1831; and to Elizabeth Hoar, the finacée of Emerson's brother Charles, who died of tuberculosis in 1836, four months before the scheduled wedding. Source: Robert D. Richardson, Jr., *Emerson: The Mind on Fire* (University of California Press, 1995).

"We Are Occasional Like That" takes its title from a line in Jack Gilbert's poem, "Music is in the Piano Only When it is Played," in *Refusing Heaven* (Alfred A Knopf, 2005).

"Ginseng on Court Street" owes a debt to Michael Brick, whose article "The Coffee was Poured with Negative Reinforcement" (*New York Times*, June 4, 2004) supplied several of the facts and details used in this poem. A few of the names and references have been changed for artistic purposes.

"In Eisenstadt, Visiting the Jewish Museum" uses statistics found in Johannes Reiss's compilation "*. . . because our love for our home town has been drained from us . . .*": *A Walk Through the Jewish History of Eisenstadt* (Österreichisches Jüdisches Museum, 2001).

About the Author

Lucia Galloway, a Pushcart Nominee and winner of the Robert Haiduke Prize, has published poems in a variety of journals, including *Columbia Poetry Review, Cumberland Poetry Review, Flyway, Gertrude, Her Mark, The Lyric, The MacGuffin, Poemeleon, Poetry Midwest, Prism Review, Redheaded Stepchild, Spillway, Thema,* and *Verdad*. She is the author of a chapbook, *Playing Outside* (Finishing Line Press, 2005). A native Illinoisan transplanted after college to California, she currently lives in Claremont, where she co-hosts the Poetry Reading Series of the Claremont Library.

Photo by J.A. Penn

www.ingramcontent.com/pod-product-compliance
Lightning Source LLC
Chambersburg PA
CBHW052111070526
44584CB00017B/2439